Pebble® Plus

First Ladies
Hillary Clinton

by Sally Lee

Consulting Editor: Gail Saunders-Smith, PhD

Consultant: Carl Sferrazza Anthony, Historian
National First Ladies' Library
Canton, Ohio

CAPSTONE PRESS
a capstone imprint

Pebble Plus is published by Capstone Press,
151 Good Counsel Drive, P.O. Box 669, Mankato, Minnesota 56002.
www.capstonepub.com

Books published by Capstone Press are manufactured with paper
containing at least 10 percent post-consumer waste.

Library of Congress Cataloging-in-Publication Data
Lee, Sally.
  Hillary Clinton / by Sally Lee.
     p. cm.—(Pebble plus. First ladies)
  Includes bibliographical references and index.
  Summary: "Simple text and photographs describe the life of Hillary Clinton"—Provided by publisher.
  ISBN 978-1-4296-5327-5 (library binding)
  1. Clinton, Hillary Rodham—Juvenile literature. 2. Presidents' spouses—United States—Biography—Juvenile
literature. 3. Women legislators—United States—Biography—Juvenile literature. 4. United States. Congress. Senate—
Biography—Juvenile literature. 5. Women presidential candidates—United States—Biography—Juvenile literature. 6.
Women cabinet officers—United States—Biography—Juvenile literature. I. Title. II. Series.
  E887.C55L44 2011
  973.929092—dc22
  [B]   2010024906

Editorial Credits
Erika L. Shores, editor; Ashlee Suker, designer; Svetlana Zhurkin, media researcher;
   Laura Manthe, production specialist

Photo Credits
Corbis/Wally McNamee, 15
Getty Images/AFP/Indranil Mukherjee, 21; Time Life Pictures/Steve Kagan, 6–7
Shutterstock/Alaettin Yildirim, 5, 7 (caption plate); antoninaart, cover (left); 1, 4–5, 8–9, 12–13, 22–23, 24 (pattern);
   Gemenacom, 5, 9, 13 (frame); Solaria, 1, 18–19
William J. Clinton Presidential Library, cover (right), 16–17; Clinton Family Historical Photographs, 5, 9, 11, 13

Note to Parents and Teachers

The First Ladies series supports national history standards related to people and culture. This
book describes and illustrates the life of Hillary Clinton. The images support early readers
in understanding the text. The repetition of words and phrases helps early readers learn new
words. This book also introduces early readers to subject-specific vocabulary words, which are
defined in the Glossary section. Early readers may need assistance to read some words and to
use the Table of Contents, Glossary, Read More, Internet Sites, and Index sections of the book.

Printed in the United States of America in North Mankato, Minnesota.
092010
005933CGS11

Table of Contents

Early Years

Hillary Clinton has always set high goals for herself. The former first lady was born October 26, 1947, in Chicago. She was Hugh and Dorothy Rodham's oldest child.

born in
Chicago

1947

Hillary in a photo taken around age 13

During Hillary's high school years,
her minister took her youth group
to churches in poor neighborhoods.
Hillary learned how badly
minorities were treated.
Hillary wanted to help them.

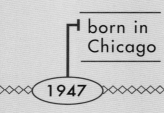

Hillary attended
Maine Township High
School South.

MAINE TOWNSHIP HIGH SCHOOL SOUTH

Young Adult

In 1969 Hillary entered
Yale Law School. She hoped
being a lawyer would help
her change things she thought
were wrong. Most lawyers
at that time were men,
but she didn't let that stop her.

born in
Chicago

1947   1969

enters Yale
Law School

Hillary met Bill Clinton at Yale.

They married in 1975.

Hillary became the first woman

lawyer at a large Arkansas law firm.

She also helped start

an organization in Arkansas

that worked for children's rights.

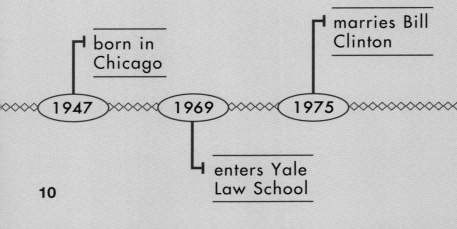

born in
Chicago

marries Bill
Clinton

1947   1969   1975

enters Yale
Law School

11

In 1979 Bill became

the governor of Arkansas.

Hillary kept her job as a lawyer.

As the state's first lady,

she helped improve schools.

In 1980 Hillary and Bill's

daughter, Chelsea, was born.

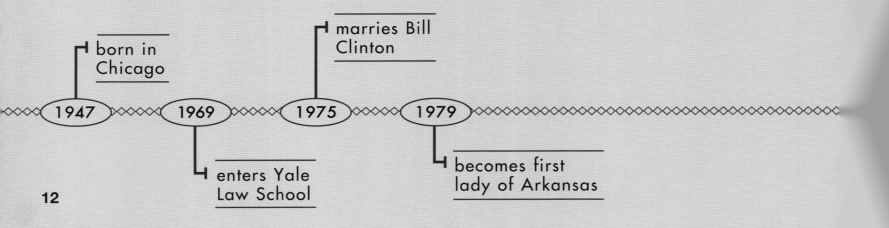

marries Bill
Clinton

born in
Chicago

1947   1969   1975   1979

enters Yale
Law School

becomes first
lady of Arkansas

13

First Lady

Bill became U.S. president in 1993. Hillary had more power than most first ladies. She led a group that tried to change how Americans received health care. Although their plan failed, it brought attention to the issue.

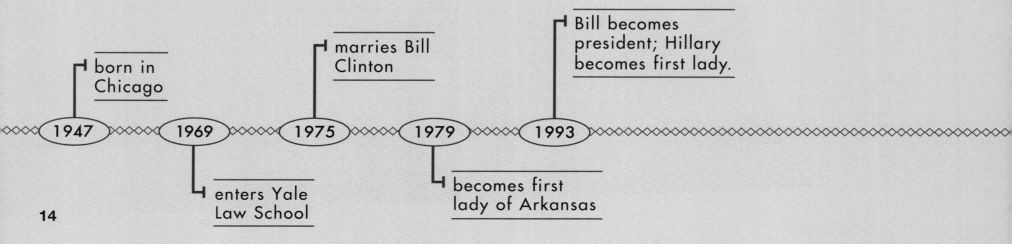

born in Chicago

marries Bill Clinton

Bill becomes president; Hillary becomes first lady.

1947   1969   1975   1979   1993

enters Yale Law School

becomes first lady of Arkansas

As the nation's first lady,
Hillary kept working for families.
She fought for health care
for poor children.
She helped change laws to
make it easier for parents
to adopt children.

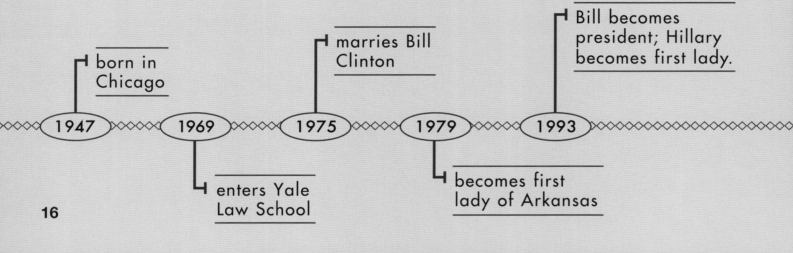

born in
Chicago

marries Bill
Clinton

Bill becomes
president; Hillary
becomes first lady.

1947   1969   1975   1979   1993

enters Yale
Law School

becomes first
lady of Arkansas

Continuing to Serve

Hillary was the first first lady to run for office herself. In 2001 she became New York's first female senator. Then she ran for U.S. president in 2008. If elected, she would become the first female president.

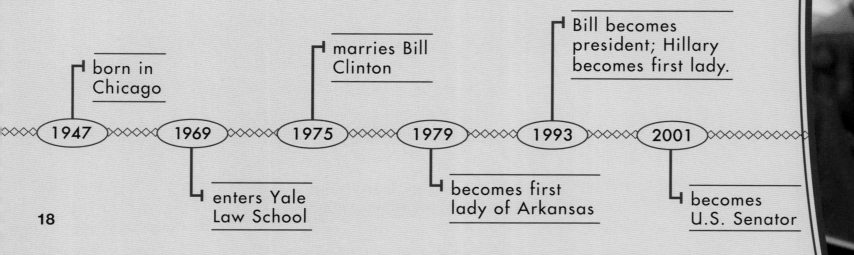

born in Chicago

enters Yale Law School

marries Bill Clinton

becomes first lady of Arkansas

Bill becomes president; Hillary becomes first lady.

becomes U.S. Senator

| 1947 | 1969 | 1975 | 1979 | 1993 | 2001 |

Hillary lost her run for president

to Barack Obama in 2008.

The president made

her secretary of state.

Hillary continues to work hard

to reach her goals and make

the country and world better.

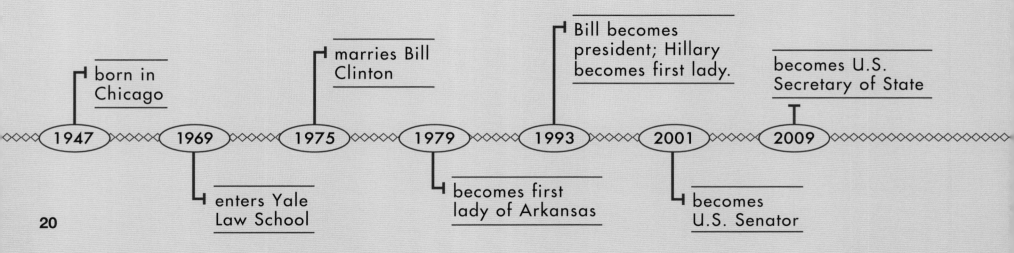

born in
Chicago

marries Bill
Clinton

Bill becomes
president; Hillary
becomes first lady.

becomes U.S.
Secretary of State

1947   1969   1975   1979   1993   2001   2009

enters Yale
Law School

becomes first
lady of Arkansas

becomes
U.S. Senator

Glossary

adopt—to make a child a legal part of a family

firm—a business made up of lawyers

lawyer—a person who is trained to advise people about the law and who acts and speaks for them in court

minister—a person who leads a church

minority—a group of people of a certain race, ethnic group, or religion living among a larger group of a different race, ethnic group, or religion

secretary of state—a person named by the president to represent the country in matters with other nations

senator—a person elected to represent the people in the government; U.S. senators serve in the Senate

Read more

Driscoll, Laura. *Hillary Clinton: An American Journey.* All Aboard Reading. New York: Grosset & Dunlap, 2008.

Krull, Kathleen. *Hillary Rodham Clinton: Dreams Taking Flight.* New York: Simon & Schuster Books for Young Readers, 2008.

Internet Sites

FactHound offers a safe, fun way to find Internet sites related to this book. All of the sites on FactHound have been researched by our staff.

Here's all you do:

Visit *www.facthound.com*

Type in this code: 9781429653275

Super-cool stuff! Check out projects, games and lots more at www.capstonekids.com

Index

Word Count: 298
Grade: 1
Early-Intervention Level: 21

24